DEADENDER

>>>>>> **Factbook:**

Jaws and Claws

>>>>>>>>>>>

Look out for the other
DEADLY books:

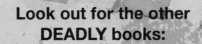

BBC EARTH

DEADLY

Factbook:
Jaws and Claws

Orion
Children's Books

First published in Great Britain in 2014
by Orion Children's Books
a division of the Orion Publishing Group Ltd
Orion House
5 Upper St Martin's Lane
London WC2H 9EA
An Hachette UK Company

1 3 5 7 9 10 8 6 4 2

Photo credits

ARDEA: 6t Ken Lucas; 19 Kenneth W. Fink; 25 Nick Gordon; 38 Ken Lucas.
BBC: 11 Charlie Bingham 2010 (from Deadly 60 Series 2); 22 Giles Badger 2010 (from Deadly 60
Series 2); 58-59 Nikki Waldron 2010 (from Deadly 60 Series 2). GETTY IMAGES: 16 Solvin Zankl;
26 Todd Gipstein; 33 Joel Sartore. MARK ROBERTS: 45. NATUREPL.COM/BBC: 13 Brandon Cole;
34-35 Eric Baccega;48 David Welling; 52 Visuals Unlimited. SHUTTERSTOCK: 28 Reptiles4all;
36 Eduardo Rivero; 42 Erwin Niemand; 43 MarcusVDT; 60 FineShine; 62 Balazska; 63 Piven
Aleksandr. THINKSTOCK: 15 Anup Shah/Photodisc; iStock: 1 & 56-57 Maria Dryfhout; 3 & 46 Lynn
Bystrom; 6b Alexomelko; 10 Lilithlita; 18 Jennifer Steck; 20-21 Mogens Trolle; 23 Eric Iseelée;
29 Musat; 30 Eric Iseelée; 31 Leopardinatree; 32 Leopardinatree; 37 MikeLane45; 40 iwikoz6;
44 Sylvie Bouchard; 50-51 Wendi Evans; 54 Krzysztof Wiktor; 55 Tanya Puntii; 66-67 Rattanapat;
68 Craykeeper; 69 Daniel Budiman; 70-71 Marshall Bruce; 72 Vladimir Melnik; 74-75 Natalia
Demidchick; 76-77 Grant Parnell. Thinkstock Fuse: 8-9; 39; 65. Thinkstock F1online: 78 Sodapix.

Compiled by Jinny Johnson   Designed by Sue Michniewicz

A catalogue record for this book is available from the British Library.

ISBN 978 1 4440 1005 3
Printed and bound in China

MIX
Paper from
responsible sources
FSC® C008047

FSC
www.fsc.org

www.orionbooks.co.uk

CONTENTS

INTRODUCTION

BABOON SKULL

For nearly all kinds of animals, jaws and claws are their main tools for attacking prey, obtaining food and defending themselves.

In this book we look at some of the extraordinary variations in animals ranging from beetles to bears and hippos to harpy eagles and the ways they use their jaws, teeth, beaks, claws and talons to survive.

STAG BEETLE

TOOTHY TERRORS

DEADLY 00

Chapter 1

The **CLOUDED LEOPARD** lives on the islands of Borneo and Sumatra and has the largest canine teeth for its skull size of any cat. They can be up to 5 centimetres long.

Canines are the big pointed teeth you can see at the front of a cat's jaws: there are 2 in the top jaw and 2 in the lower jaw. These teeth help the clouded leopard catch and kill animals such as deer, monkeys, birds and porcupines.

The clouded leopard is also a remarkably good climber and can run headfirst down tree trunks and hang upside down from branches. It swims well too.

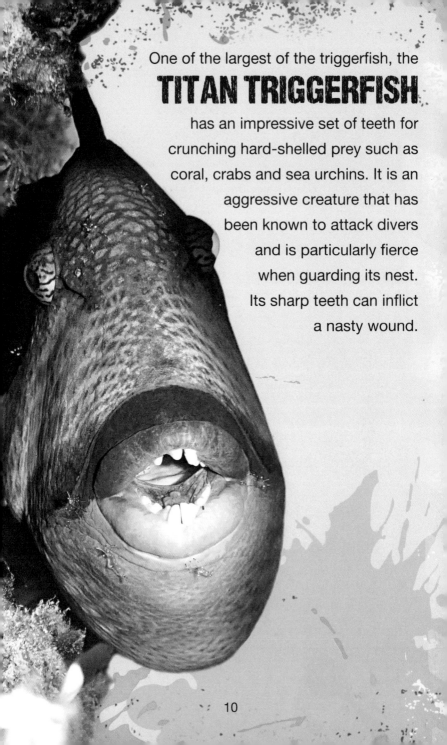

One of the largest of the triggerfish, the

TITAN TRIGGERFISH

has an impressive set of teeth for crunching hard-shelled prey such as coral, crabs and sea urchins. It is an aggressive creature that has been known to attack divers and is particularly fierce when guarding its nest. Its sharp teeth can inflict a nasty wound.

LIONS, like other cats, have 4 big canine teeth at the front of the jaws – 2 at the top and 2 at the bottom. They also have powerful jaw muscles for attacking their prey. Once a lion has brought down its victim, it will often kill it with a bite to the throat, holding on until the animal suffocates.

Between the canine teeth a cat has smaller teeth called incisors and larger teeth farther back called carnassials. The carnassials are used for cutting and slicing flesh.

A speedy streamlined killer, the

GREAT WHITE SHARK

has some of the most impressive teeth in the
animal kingdom. Its massive jaws are equipped
with as many as 300 teeth, which can be up
7.5 centimetres long. The teeth are arranged in
several rows. Those in the first 2 rows are used
for attacking prey and if any are lost, teeth from
the rows behind move into place so the shark
is never without its deadly weapons.

The teeth have serrated edges
like bread knives, which help the
great white shark cut through flesh
more quickly.

The shark has super senses, too, for detecting
prey. An injured animal has no chance as the
great white can detect tiny amounts of blood in
water. In fact, this shark could smell a drop of
blood in a billion drops of water.

BABOONS are among the largest of all monkeys. Like most of the others, they eat lots of plant food but these big-toothed creatures also prey on birds, reptiles and other small creatures.

Male baboons have massive canine teeth that they bare in a ferocious grin to threaten other males.

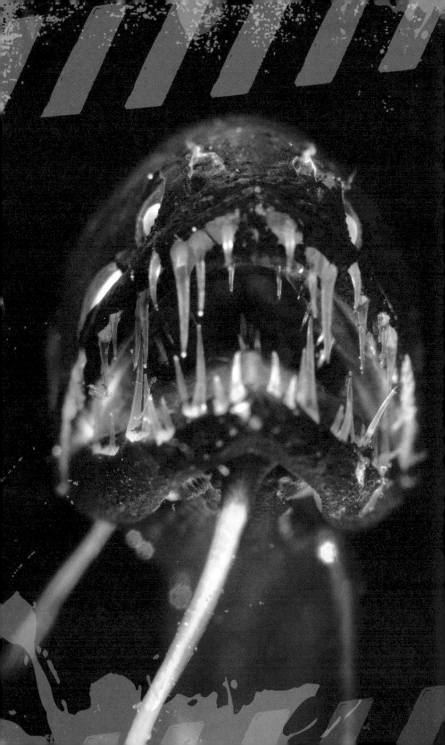

The fearsome
looking female

BLACK DRAGONFISH

has a terrifying array
of fang-like teeth in its
gaping jaws, which it uses
to snap up shrimp and
smaller fish.

The dragonfish lives in the
darkness of the deep sea
but can make its own light.
It has light organs called
photophores on its body
and these produce light
that includes infra-red to
help the fish find prey in
total darkness.

True to their big cat namesake,

LEOPARD SEALS

are ferocious hunters and they prey on other seals as well as fish, penguins and squid.

A leopard seal has a large head and its strong jaws are equipped with scarily efficient teeth. These include long sharp canines and incisors used for gripping prey and tearing flesh apart, as well as molars (cheek teeth). These molars interlock to form a sort of trap for catching smaller fish and shrimp.

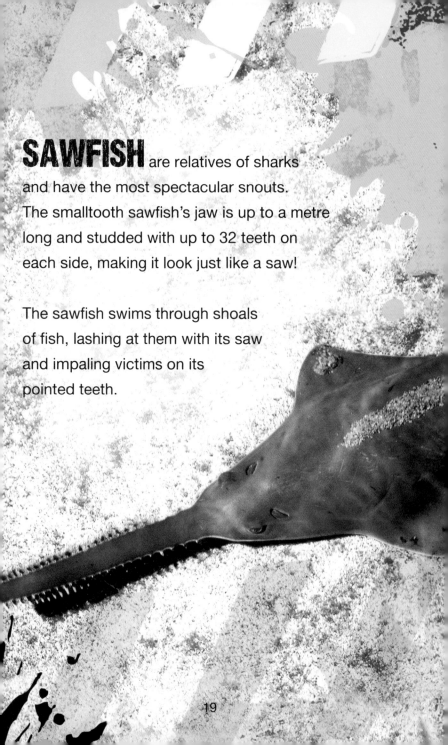

SAWFISH are relatives of sharks
and have the most spectacular snouts.
The smalltooth sawfish's jaw is up to a metre
long and studded with up to 32 teeth on
each side, making it look just like a saw!

The sawfish swims through shoals
of fish, lashing at them with its saw
and impaling victims on its
pointed teeth.

The **SALTWATER CROCODILE** has the most powerful bite of any crocodile. Scientists in Florida tested 83 alligators and crocodiles with a special piece of kit that measures the force of an animal's bite in pounds per square inch. The champions were saltwater crocodiles, which registered a force of 3,700 pounds per square inch (psi). The croc's incredible jaw power enables it to chomp through any prey that comes its way.

In comparison, lions and tigers have a bite force of about 1,000 psi and humans only 150–200.

You might be surprised to hear that the toothy jaws of crocodiles and alligators are extremely sensitive. Thousands of tiny bumps on the jaws pick up the smallest movement of prey in the water and the reptile reacts in a fraction of a second.

These super-sensitive organs can even tell a prey animal from a floating log.

PIRANHAS are relatively small fish but their tightly packed teeth and strong jaws make them formidable hunters. The teeth are triangular in shape and the bottom row of teeth fit exactly into the spaces between the teeth in the top row. This makes a super-efficient biting tool – a bit like a bear trap.

Piranhas sometimes hunt in groups and attack creatures larger than themselves. More often they go it alone, catching other fish as well as shellfish.

STRIPED HYENAS

are scavengers. That means that they will eat animals that have died naturally or been killed and left by other hunters. A hyena's jaws and 34 teeth are well suited to its scavenging habits. They are extra-strong and powerful, enabling the hyena to crunch through bones and other tough body parts that other predators might not be able to tackle.

Striped hyenas sometimes kill prey for themselves, such as hares and rats, and they eat insects and fruit. They will also steal scraps of food from rubbish heaps.

Bats can have up to 38 teeth but the

COMMON VAMPIRE BAT

has only 20. The bat does not need as many teeth as other bats because it feeds only on blood so does not have to chew its meal. However, the teeth it does have are extra deadly. To obtain its meal, the bat climbs up on to a warm-blooded animal, such as a horse, and shaves away the hair from a patch of skin. It makes a wound about the size of your little fingernail with its viciously sharp teeth, then laps up the blood that flows.

Vampire bats cannot survive more than 2 or 3 days without a blood meal. A bat will regurgitate blood to another member of its colony who has not managed to hunt successfully.

The **PAYARA**, also known as the vampire tetra, is a freshwater fish, which lives in the Amazon basin. It grows more than a metre long and has 2 huge fangs in its lower jaw that can measure as much as 10 centimetres – that's more than an adult human's finger. A fierce hunter, it preys on other fish – and people say it may eat piranhas!

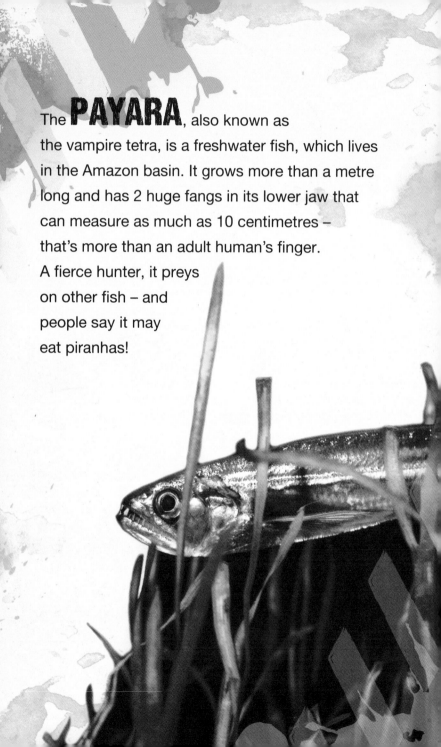

SPECIAL ADAPTATIONS

Chapter 2

The **ALLIGATOR SNAPPING TURTLE** is one of the largest freshwater turtles. This huge turtle can weigh 80 kilograms – more than an average adult human.

Its mighty beak-like jaws are a lethal weapon. But the turtle also has a clever trick – it lures prey close by displaying a little bit of pink flesh that hangs in its mouth and looks just like a juicy worm to a fish. When the hungry fish comes to investigate the possible meal, the turtle snaps its jaws shut, trapping the fish or even slicing it in two.

In the insect world, the

ASSASSIN BUG

is a deadly hunter.

It has special piercing mouthparts, which it uses to stab prey such as aphids and other bugs. It injects a substance that dissolves the victim's body tissues and then sucks up its meal.

The **AARDVARK**'s favourite prey is ants and termites and its long snout and strong claws are the perfect tools for finding its food. This shy, nocturnal animal snuffles about in search of a column of ants on the march and it can break down a termite mound with ease, using its spoon-shaped claws. It gobbles up its prey with its sticky tongue, which can measure up to 30 centimetres, and it can eat more than 50,000 insects a night.

The big claws, 4 on the front feet and 5 on each back foot, also allow the aardvark to dig burrows for shelter during the day. The aardvark lives in southern Africa and its name means 'earth pig' in the Afrikaans language.

Claws are hugely important for all cats – from lions to your pet kitten. Cats use their claws for catching and holding on to struggling prey, for climbing and also to defend themselves from enemies.

CHEETAH PAW

Most cats have claws that are retractable – held back in special fleshy sheaths inside the toes. This keeps them out of the way and protects them from wear and tear. But when needed, the sharp claws can be extended in a fraction of a second. They have hooked tips that sink into prey and they are very hard to remove.

CHEETAHS are the only cats that do not have semi-retractable claws. The cheetah is the fastest running of all land mammals and needs its claws for grip when moving at speed.

The **GREY HERON** has a long dagger-like beak that makes a perfect food-gathering tool.

The heron often stands in water, watching for fish. When it spots something it makes a lightning-fast strike with its beak, sometimes stabbing the prey several times. It then snatches its meal from the water. Herons are big birds with a wingspan of up to 1.75 metres.

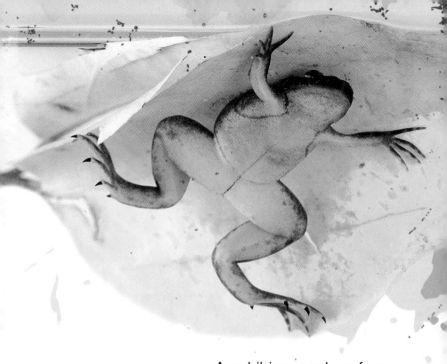

Amphibians such as frogs
don't usually have claws but the

AFRICAN CLAWED FROG

does appear to have little claws on 3 of the toes
on each back foot. In fact, these are not true
claws but hardened tips on the toes,
which it uses to tear its food apart.

These frogs are up to 12 centimetres long.
They are scavengers and eat any dead or
dying animals they can find. They also attack
other small creatures such as tadpoles, insects
and fish.

Although **BROWN BEARS** feed mostly on nuts, fruit, leaves and roots, they do have massive claws and sharp teeth. Their claws are 5-10 centimetres – as long or longer than an adult human's finger.

The bear uses its claws for digging up roots and other food but they can cause severe wounds if it does attack another animal. The claws also come in useful for catching salmon – an important food for the bears in some areas. Brown bears do occasionally catch larger animals such as moose and elk.

A full-grown brown bear can be 2.4 metres long and weigh over 500 kilograms – that's more than 8 average people!

The **RIGHT WHALE** has an enormous head, which makes up about a third of its 18-metre body. The whale's massive jaws do not contain teeth but large plates made of a hair-like substance called baleen. About 225 of these plates hang from each upper jaw and act like a giant sieve.

The whale uses them to filter small items of food, such as tiny shrimp-like creatures, from the water.

As its name suggests, the **SNAIL KITE**'s favourite food is snails and it has the perfect beak for the job.

The snail kite is a bird of prey, which usually lives near water and feeds mainly on a kind of freshwater snail called the apple snail. The kite scoops its prey from the water with its clawed feet and carries it away to a safe perch. Holding the snail in one foot and standing on the other, the kite inserts its long curved slender beak into the shell. It extracts the juicy flesh of the snail with the help of the hooked tip of its beak.

The **LAMPREY** looks like a fish but strictly speaking it is not a fish at all but a primitive type of vertebrate animal. It is sometimes known as a jawless fish because it has no true jaws. Instead it has a kind of sucking disc at the front of the head, which contains rows of lots of little pointed teeth.

The lamprey attaches itself to the side of a fish with this disc, rasps away some skin and then feeds on the victim.

The lamprey has a slender body like an eel and can grow over a metre long.

The **FLAMINGO** has one of the most unusual beaks of any bird. The beak is lined with rows of tiny hair-like structures and used to filter food from the water.

The long-legged flamingo stands in water and bends its neck so it can hold its beak upside down under the surface. It sucks water or mud into its beak, then pushes it out at the sides with its fleshy tongue. Any tiny food items such as shrimp are caught on the filtering structures and then swallowed by the flamingo.

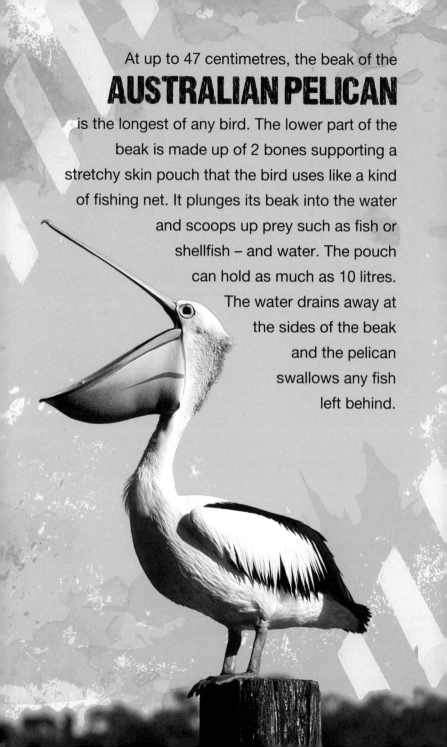

At up to 47 centimetres, the beak of the

AUSTRALIAN PELICAN

is the longest of any bird. The lower part of the beak is made up of 2 bones supporting a stretchy skin pouch that the bird uses like a kind of fishing net. It plunges its beak into the water and scoops up prey such as fish or shellfish – and water. The pouch can hold as much as 10 litres. The water drains away at the sides of the beak and the pelican swallows any fish left behind.

DEADLY HUNTERS

Chapter 3

The **HONEY BADGER** might sound cute but it certainly isn't. This fierce little carnivore is less than a metre long but is well known for punching above its weight. Some claim it is the world's most fearless animal.

The honey badger preys mainly on birds, insects and reptiles but it will attack much bigger animals, even antelopes and buffalo, to defend itself. It has a sturdy body with a large head for its size and strong jaws and teeth. On its front feet are powerful claws, which it uses to dig into burrows when it is pursuing prey.

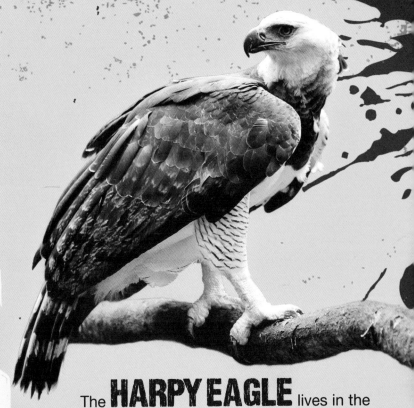

The **HARPY EAGLE** lives in the Amazon rainforest and is one of the biggest and strongest of all birds of prey. It hunts animals such as monkeys and sloths, chasing them through the jungle trees. It snatches up its victims with sharp talons, which can be up to 13 centimetres. In fact, the harpy's talons can be longer than a grizzly bear's claws! The eagle then tears its meal apart with its awesome hooked beak.

The harpy's wings measure 2 metres from tip to tip when fully spread.

POLAR BEARS are huge

animals and they have equally huge paws, measuring 30 centimetres across – the size of a dinner plate. These paws are equipped with curved claws, up to 5 centimetres long, which the bear uses for seizing prey and for getting a grip on the ice in its Arctic home.

A polar bear has 42 strong teeth for attacking prey and slicing through flesh.

A spider's jaws are called chelicerae and are positioned at the front of the body. The jaws are tipped with fangs and in most spiders these fangs are connected to venom glands. The spider uses its jaws to seize its prey and hold it while it injects venom.

The GOLIATH BIRD-EATING SPIDER

has fangs as big as a cheetah's claws – they are up to 2.5 centimetres long and they're extremely sharp. This spider doesn't make a web but instead pounces on its victims and attacks with its fangs and venom. It does kill birds but more often preys on insects, lizards and even mice and snakes.

The **BALD EAGLE** has immensely strong talons, which it uses to catch its favourite food – fish. Having spotted its prey from the air, the eagle swoops over the water surface and grasps the fish in its talons, which lock around the prey. Lots of little spikes called spicules on the underside of the toes help it grasp its slippery meals.

An eagle cannot chew its food so it uses its massive hooked beak to tear its meal to pieces.

Bald eagles hunt land animals such as squirrels and rats too and eat carrion. They will also steal food from other birds.

By the way, the bald eagle isn't really bald. Its head is covered with white feathers.

The biggest of all wild dogs,

GREY WOLVES

are awesome hunters with powerful crushing jaws and sharp-clawed feet.

A wolf's jaws are lined with 42 strong teeth, which can crunch though bone as well as flesh. A wolf can eat as much as 10 kilograms of meat at a sitting – that's like us eating 5 legs of lamb for dinner!

Wolves live in packs and keep in touch with blood-curdling howls that can be heard more than 9 kilometres away.

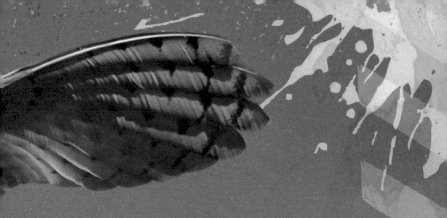

Sharp-clawed talons are the

BARN OWL's

deadly weapons. Its feet are extra strong and on each are 4 toes, all equipped with a vicious hooked claw. The underside of the foot has a ridged surface that helps the owl keep hold of struggling prey, such as rats, mice and rabbits.

When the owl is in flight, 3 of its 4 toes face forward and one back. But when attacking prey another of the front toes is turned to the back, giving the owl the ideal vice-like gripping tool.

A giant lizard, the **KOMODO DRAGON** looks like it belongs to the age of the dinosaurs. It preys on creatures such deer, buffalo and wild pigs and will also take carrion – animals that are already dead.

The dragon's jaws contain venom glands. As the dragon bites its victim, this venom enters the animal's wounds. Even if the prey does briefly manage to escape the dragon's clutches it soon dies.

A male komodo can measure up to 3 metres and weigh over 130 kilograms.

ARMY ANTS are tiny but they travel in troops of many thousands so make an awesome force. Together they can overcome prey many times their own size, such as scorpions and caterpillars.

As the army marches through the forest attacking anything in their path and stinging it to death, special soldier ants act as guards to the rest. Army ants have powerful jaws, called mandibles, and those of the soldiers are particularly big.

In fact rainforest tribes have been known to use these strong-jawed insects to clamp wounds together – Nature's version of stitches!

The **JAGUAR** lives in forests in Central and South America and is the third largest cat, after tigers and lions. It has an extremely powerful bite and can kill its prey by piercing the skull with its sharp teeth. It hunts anything from cattle to fish and lizards and can even crack though a tortoise's hard shell.

The jaguar's name comes from its local Indian name – yaguara, which means 'a beast that kills its prey with one bound'. This gives you a good idea of this big cat's hunting skill!

The **TASMANIAN DEVIL** is a hunter and scavenger with a ferocious bite. A strong, stocky creature, it weighs about as much as a small dog but its head is large for its body and its jaws are among the most powerful of any animal.

This creature munches up whatever food it can find and can crunch through anything, including fur and bones! Devils also feed on carrion. They live only on the island of Tasmania, off the coast of Australia.

RATTLESNAKE jaws are an ideal prey-catching tool. The 2 halves of the jaw are loosely attached so can open extra wide to engulf large prey. Inside the mouth are 2 sharp fangs, which lie flat when not in use.

When the snake opens its mouth wide to attack, the fangs swing into position. As the snake strikes and plunges its fangs into its victim, poison is pumped through the hollow fangs and injected into the prey.

The eastern diamondback rattlesnake is the largest of the rattlesnakes and the biggest venomous snake in North America. The longest-known diamondback measured 2.4 metres.

This huge **BOA CONSTRICTOR** does not have a venomous bite but instead squeezes its prey to death! It wraps its body around its victim and holds it so tight that the prey cannot breathe and soon dies.

The boa can kill prey much larger than itself this way and because of its special jaws it can eat them too. The boa's jaws are super-flexible and can open enormously wide to swallow animals such as pigs, which are much bigger than the boa's head.

The boa, like all snakes, cannot chew but simply swallows its prey whole. The meal is then slowly broken down and digested once inside the snake's body. The digestion process can take 6 days.

A full-grown boa can be as much as 3 metres long.

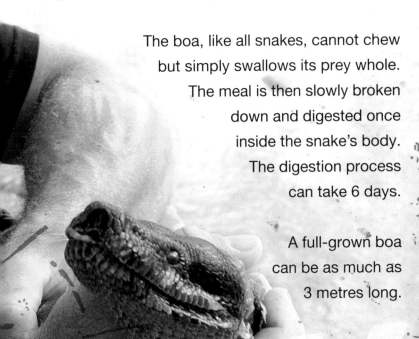

ORCAS, also known as killer whales, are some of the fiercest hunters in the sea and prey on fish, birds, seals and even other whales. Their huge jaws are lined with about 50 teeth that can be up to 10 centimetres long.

These highly intelligent animals hunt in groups, called pods, and work together to catch their prey. They use clever techniques such as creating waves to wash a basking seal off an ice floe and into the water where they can attack it.

A full-grown male orca weighs as much as 9,000 kilograms and grows up to 9.7 metres – more than twice the length of an average car. Females are smaller. The dorsal fin, the large fin on an orca's back, can measure 1.8 metres – the height of a tall adult person. The shape of the fin is slightly different in each orca so a good way of identifying individual whales.

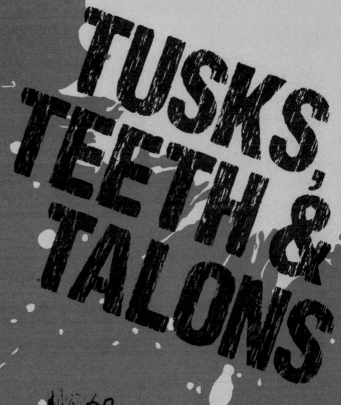

TUSKS, TEETH & TALONS

DEADLY

Chapter 4

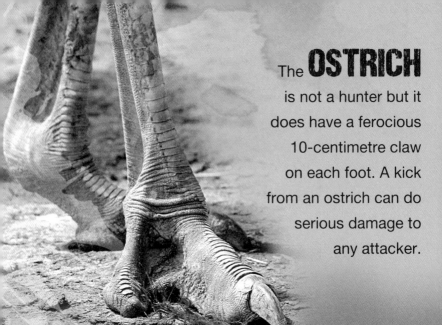

The **OSTRICH** is not a hunter but it does have a ferocious 10-centimetre claw on each foot. A kick from an ostrich can do serious damage to any attacker.

This strange bird is the tallest and heaviest of all birds. It also has the biggest eyes of any land animal – they are up to 5 centimetres across. Ostriches cannot fly but they run fast – up to 70 kilometres an hour for short distances.

The ostrich feeds mostly on plant material, such as seeds and leaves, but may also gobble up insects and other small creatures.

An **ELEPHANT**'s tusks are actually very big incisor teeth. Both male and female African elephants have tusks and they keep growing throughout the animal's life. The longest tusks ever known were more than 3 metres. The elephant also has a large head to support its heavy trunk, tusks and jaws.

Elephants use their tusks to strip bark from trees, to uproot other plants to eat and for defending themselves from enemies. Males also use their tusks in battles with one another over females.

African elephants are the biggest living land animals. A male African elephant can weigh up to 6 tonnes – more than 4 average cars. The female is smaller, about half the weight of the male.

The **HIPPOPOTAMUS** is not a predator but it is one of the most dangerous animals in Africa. It's also one of the biggest of all land animals. The hippo is built like a tank and can weigh up to 3,200 kilograms – that's more than 45 people. The largest known hippo weighed 4,500 kilograms! Its enormous mouth opens over a metre wide and contains king-size teeth that may measure as much as 40 or 50 centimetres. These giant teeth are used by rival males to threaten one another and as weapons in fights.

Males fight over territory and take part in fierce battles. The winner marks his new kingdom by lifting his tail and using it to scatter poo and wee over as wide an area as he can.

Hippos spend most of the day in water keeping cool. They come out on land at night to feed, mostly on grass.

The male **FIDDLER CRAB** has one claw that is much larger than the other. The crab uses this claw to attract females with waving displays and to defend his burrow from rival males.

These crabs live in tropical regions and scientists think that the big claws help them lose heat and keep cool on scorching beaches. This means a crab can stay out in the open longer without overheating when trying to attract females with his claw displays.

Bizarre **BABIRUSAS** belong to the pig family of mammals and live in tropical rainforests in Southeast Asia.

The males have curious curved tusks, which are actually extra-long canine teeth. The upper canines, which may measure as much as 30 centimetres, extend through the animal's snout and curve back over the face. The shorter lower canines also stick out from the jaw.

The tusks look threatening but in fact the babirusa uses its lower, shorter tusks for fighting. The long tusks break too easily.

The **HOATZIN** is a strange-looking bird that lives in the Amazon rainforest. Young hoatzins have hook-like claws on their wings that help the bird clamber about in the trees to escape predators before they are able to fly. These claws are lost by the time the hoatzin has grown into an adult.

The hoatzin's claws probably look like those on the wings of *Archaeopteryx*, which lived thousands of years ago. *Archaeopteryx* was one of the first known birds.

Hoatzins are sometimes known as 'stinkbirds' because they are extraordinarily smelly! This is because they feed mostly on leaves, which ferment inside the body.

The **WALRUS** is a relative of seals and sea lions but has huge tusks. These can be up to a metre long – that's twice as long as an adult person's arm. The tusks are actually immense canine teeth that grow throughout the walrus's life.

A walrus doesn't use its tusks for obtaining food but for fighting rivals, breaking through ice and even hooking on to an ice floe to keep itself safe while sleeping. It can also fend off polar bears with its tusks.

This big creature, which can weigh up to 1,500 kilograms, feeds mostly on small prey such as clams, mussels, shrimps and fish.

STAG BEETLES get their name from the male's giant jaws, which look rather like a deer's antlers. The male stag beetle uses these jaws, called mandibles, in impressive wrestling matches with other males to win territory or mates. In Britain a full-grown male stag beetle is about 7.5 centimetres long, but elsewhere in the world these beetles can measure up to 12 centimetres. Females are shorter with smaller jaws.

A **CAMEL** is a plant eater but it has a fearsome set of teeth that could do serious damage to anyone unlucky enough to get in their way.

There are 34 teeth in all in a camel's jaws
and they are designed to crunch through the
toughest desert plants.

Unlike most plant-eaters, which have only
broad flat teeth for crushing their food,
the camel also has sharp fang-like
teeth at the front of its jaws.

Everyone knows that birds don't have teeth but a type of duck called the

MERGANSER makes you wonder.

Its beak has serrated edges – like a bread knife – and looks remarkably toothy.

The merganser feeds on fish and this special beak helps it grip its prey.

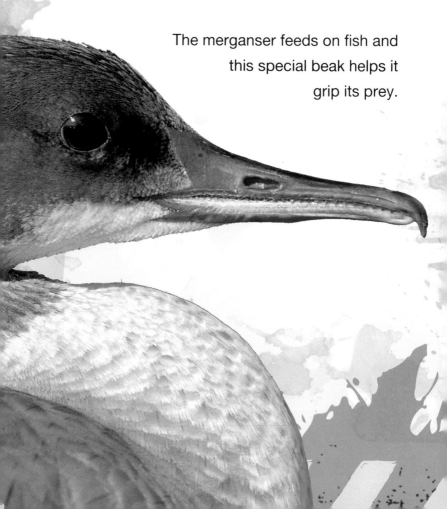

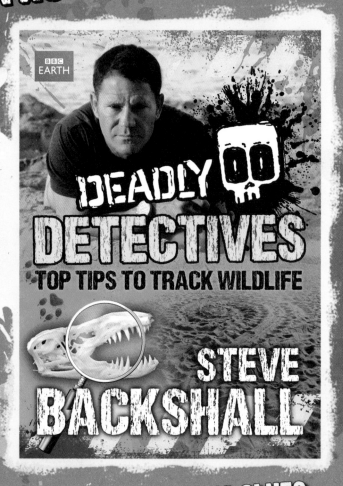